IS THERE A SAMSON
IN YOU?

IS THERE A SAMSON IN YOU?

✦

AN HONEST LOOK INTO THE MIRROR OF MALE BONDAGE

H. Ronald Roseboro

iUniverse, Inc.
New York   Bloomington

IS THERE A SAMSON IN YOU?
AN HONEST LOOK INTO THE MIRROR OF MALE BONDAGE

iUniverse books may be ordered through booksellers or by contacting:

iUniverse
1663 Liberty Drive
Bloomington, IN 47403
www.iuniverse.com
1-800-Authors (1-800-288-4677)

Because of the dynamic nature of the Internet, any Web addresses or links contained in this book may have changed since publication and may no longer be valid.

ISBN: 978-1-4502-1153-6 (sc)
ISBN: 978-0-595-89248-8 (ebk)

Printed in the United States of America

iUniverse rev. date: 3/3/2010

Dedication

This book is dedicated to men who have an earnest desire for change . . . and

To those who find themselves stalled at the intersection of Boyhood Street and Manhood Lane, and . . .

. . . to our women who have suffered long with us, been hurt by us, encouraged us, rebuked us, and who believed in us, even when we did not possess the faith to believe in ourselves.

It is written for those who struggle with inner conflicts, pain, fear, and the warfare that rages within their souls.

I honor and dedicate this book to all who toil with honor and dedication within the healing community: Clinical Counselors, Pastors, Deliverance Ministers, Life Coaches, Civil and Human rights activists, and Mentors.

This book is also dedicated to those who are committed to seeing men take their rightful position by getting into position!

Contents

Introduction

Regardless of whether you are a seminary student, Bible scholar, historical Guru, or illiterate, you have no doubt heard the story of Samson and Delilah, for it has been echoed throughout time and passed down from generation to generation. You can ask anyone a Bible Trivia question concerning who Delilah's victim was, and I am sure that the unanimous answer would be, "Samson."

Samson was well known and hailed for his superhuman strength. However, like many men today, Samson was a He-man with a She-weakness. Oftentimes men suffer in the silence of their own personal midnight struggles. It is unthinkable for a man who possesses a high level of power (whether that power derives from social status, wealth, business success, or even church hierarchy) to be made powerless and rendered helpless by a Delilah.

The life of Samson serves as both a testimony and template of secrecy and inner oppression within the hearts of many men. Unlike many Bible stories, the story of Samson speaks volumes to the concealed conflict that most men endure and are held hostage by. I believe that Samson's inner struggle was very real and is relevant to men today. Society tends to "play down" issues by simply ruling habitual male struggles as, "Just a passing phase, everyone makes mistakes," or "a man will be a man." However, chronic conflicts that afflict the souls of men cannot be overlooked or ignored. Society concludes that men are weak if they pursue clinical counseling, gain faith in God, or acquire help in their time of emotional need. Therefore, men tend to medicate themselves through alcohol abuse, drugs, sex, pornography, working excessive hours at the office, and using many other techniques to take away the pain and shame of the Samson within.

The hard cold truth is: there is a Samson in all of us. There is a vice or issue in each one of us that we fiercely combat. Everyone's struggle is unique and tailor made for them. Men that share in the heated warfare of inner issues like Samson are silently screaming for help. We see them quite often, but without spiritual glasses that enable us to see deeply into another's soul, it is hard to detect and difficult to provide help. They are business tycoons, doctors, attorneys, politicians, pastors, teachers, fathers, husbands, sons, athletes, entertainers, and students. They cross all ethnic and racial barriers, and exist in all levels of society, including tax brackets. I feel that as our men begin the process of healing and become empowered through spiritual freedom, our women and children will follow suit.

The time has come to break the chains of male bondage.

CHAPTER 1

A MAN, A MANDATE, A MISSION

Every man will experience his own moment of truth and the opportunity to stare manhood in the face and see it for what it is and not what it appears to be.

I can remember being a young boy, traveling with my father to visit his family in Rock Hill, South Carolina. During the fall, I always looked forward to the county fair. Going to the fair with my cousins was always an enjoyable time of fun and adolescent freedom from the company and discipline of boring adults. We ran until either fatigue or an officer of the law slowed us down! And because of the limited choice of rides, we rode the same roller coaster for hours, again and again, until our pockets were empty. However, one of my favorite fair activities was the house of mirrors. The house of mirrors was an enclosed area that was filled with mirror-like grids made from a compound called convex. Convex derives from the Latin word convexus which means arch. This is why the mirrors in the house had a bowl or curb like appearance. The convex mirrors provided obstacles for the participants and unusual yet confusing reflections of themselves. As I attempted to find my way out of the maze, laughter would erupt like a volcano from kids that saw funny reflections of themselves and others. Years later, as an adult, when I reentered the house of mirrors I had a completely different perspective of what I was seeing. I began to think how we are perceived as men and how we perceive ourselves. When I walked through the maze of mirrors I saw different variations of myself as a man. In one mirror I saw myself as handsome, ugly in another, fat in another, and skinny in yet another mirror. The list of distortions went on and on. I couldn't help but think about society and the many things that

1

are taught to men: to believe what is masculine and manly, or the things that make us unattractive, flawed, or weak in the eyes of others and thus ourselves. Why are we so displeased with who we are as men? We are the only original copy of ourselves yet we constantly attempt to become something that we are not. What are the mirrors in our lives that we have perceived ourselves through based on the perceptions and ideas of others, and why do we believe these distortions? And in many cases why have we actually *become* the lie? When a lie is believed, it is given life and it becomes empowered. However, when a lie is not believed, it dies. I have come to realize that I can shatter the mirrors and the original copy will still be me, but the shattered pieces of public perception will have no power.

The courageous, victorious, and tragic life of Samson begins in the book of Judges, Chapters 13 through 16. Samson's name in Hebrew means sunshine. Families and communities from the Eastern cultures believe that a child's name serves as identification and a testimony of the child. Therefore, Samson's divine birth from the womb of a barren woman was Jehovah's plan for providing sunshine (or rays of hope) to the Israelites who were at that time suffering under the dark oppression of the Philistines. The brutal Philistine oppression upon the Israelites came as a result of disobedience, idolatry, and harlotry. From the time of Moses, the Israelites had found a perverse enjoyment in serving the pagan gods of surrounding nations and following their lewd lifestyle. For this reason, the God of Israel painfully allowed his chosen children to suffer at the hands of the ones that they wanted to mimic.

> **"They forsook the LORD and served baal and the ashtoreths. And the anger of the LORD was hot against Israel. So He delivered them into the hands of plunderers who despoiled them; and He sold them into the hands of their enemies all around, so that they could no longer stand before their enemies." (Judges 2:13-14).**

Nevertheless, because of the compassion, love, and mercy of God, He would constantly send them relief and deliverance, despite the hardness of their hearts.

> **"And when the LORD raised up judges for them, the LORD was with the judge and delivered them out of the hand of their enemies all the days of the judge; for the LORD was moved to pity by their groaning because of those who oppressed them and harassed them. And**

it came to pass, when the judge was dead, that they reverted and behaved more corruptly than their fathers, by following other gods, to serve them and bow down to them. They did not cease from their own doings nor from their stubborn way." (Judges 2:18-19)

The name of the book Judges reflects the position of God's selected messengers, who were sent by Him to be Judges, instituting justice and retribution on behalf of God's people. Samson was one of many judges throughout time that was anointed and appointed to successfully complete three specific missions for God:

1. Provoke the Israelites to repentance and return to the one and true living God.
2. Execute justice through legal and civil matters.
3. Repay God's enemies and the oppressors of His people for oppression and enslavement.

Therefore, from a cliché perspective, Samson was a man who wore many hats. He was a pastor (spiritual advocate), a judge (legal advocate), and an abolitionist (civil and human rights advocate). Samson was not some dumb muscle head; he was highly intelligent and analytical in his thinking. He was a man who was given three specific missions and a mandate to be a faithful Nazarite.

To fully understand and appreciate the role of a Nazarite as well as the functions of one you will have to visit the book of Numbers, chapter 6. There you will find God's order and expectations concerning everyone who takes the vow of a Nazarite. Nazarites were individuals who desired a deeper and more intimate relationship with God. Therefore, they separated themselves to God for at least 60 days. During this time of sanctification and purification, they were to drink no wine, nor cut their hair, and they were forbidden from polluting themselves by touching a dead body. These strict regulations were given to promote a much deeper spiritual meaning and lifestyle for the Nazarite.

God knew that certain devices would enslave his electorate:

"Harlotry, wine, and new wine enslave the heart." (Hosea 4:11).

It was God's intention that the 60-day boot camp process would be extended to a life long act of service and sanctification for the Nazarite. God also wanted to instill self-restraint and discipline within each Nazarite. And finally, it was God's plan to teach the Nazarite to live a pure life of holiness. Purity is the secret ingredient for integrity. Therefore, to remain in a state of purity, God commanded them not to touch any dead thing. From a biological view, a person could become sick or even die from having close contact with a dead body. However, from a spiritual viewpoint, a person could become spiritually diseased or suffer moral death by intimately associating with someone who is spiritually dead. A spiritually dead person is physically alive but spiritually and morally dead. God had high yet attainable expectations for Nazarites. They were like spiritual Navy Seals within a platoon of soldiers. Nazarites were groomed to be God's elite Special Forces unit that could be called into a spiritual war zone at any time to overthrow and destroy any enemy. The interesting thing concerning Numbers chapter 6 is the process of becoming a Nazarite. It is predicated upon one taking a vow to God and separating himself for God. The chapter clearly echoes that the person interested in becoming a Nazarite must separate himself. However, for the first time in recorded history, Samson was the only man who did not take it upon himself to become a Nazarite, but rather God ordained him to be a Nazarite from his mother's womb.

> **"For behold, you shall conceive and bear a son. And no razor shall come upon his head, for the child shall be a Nazarite to God from the womb; and he shall begin to deliver Israel out of the hand of the Philistines." (Judges 13:5)**

This is pivotal to understanding the significance and purpose that God had for Samson; while others took great liberty to become spiritual Navy Seals, Samson was created *from an embryo* to be a spiritual Navy Seal. This is a clear indication that Samson as a Nazarite was divinely appointed to be of a higher spiritual rank, greater level of anointing, sharper discernment, and a closer relationship with God compared to other Nazarites. He was a spiritual general among corporals and captains. This also shows us how much of a threat he was to the kingdom of satan and the system of the world. For this reason, it is obvious to conclude that God had a divine plan for Samson, but satan had a plan of demise for Samson. When God created the soul and spirit of Samson to become a Nazarite general, his strengths and weaknesses were already calculated within the plan of God. However, it did not take satan long to learn about the DNA of Samson by understanding his strengths as well as his weaknesses. Therefore, it was fitting for satan to plan a strategy of attack against Samson based on classified information that had now become public information. Samson prematurely died as a young man at the age of forty. Samson self-destructed in the summer of his life. He was created to deliver a nation, but he spent forty years trying to deliver himself.

The Three M's

It is extremely important for every man to know the answer to the questions: What is a *Man*? What is his *Mandate*? And what is his *Mission*?

These are the three m's of maturity. A man knows and accepts who he is. A mandate is to know what he is to do — his purpose on Earth. A mission is to know what to do with what you have. I believe the three m's will add to our maturity, focus of vision, and self-restraint.

Here is the million-dollar question: How many of us can honestly say that we know what our mandate is, and what our mission is? If we don't find the answers to these questions and do it, it is highly possible that our lives will parallel the life and death of Samson. As a man, have you ever been in hot pursuit of something or someone that had nothing to do with the three m's in your life? Now I know I'm not the only one that's willing to step on Front Street. In fact, if I could count how many times I chased the wind, Front Street would be my home. Oftentimes we foolishly waste days, weeks, months, and even years, doing the opposite of what we were purposed to do. This occurs because either we don't know who we are, what to do, or what to do with what we have. Or maybe we know these things, but refuse to do them. Regardless of our reason, our lack of knowledge kills us.

"My people are destroyed from lack of knowledge." (Hosea 4:6)

You maybe silently asking, "How do I find out who I am, and why am I here?"

I believe that the answer lies in asking the one who created you, which is God, and asking yourself a profound question: "What job or career would I be willing to work for free because of the peace and fulfillment that I gain from it?"

It is also quite possible to be great at more than one thing or to have multiple gifts and talents. However, you can only effectively do one task at a time. This does not mean that you can never do more than one thing, but rather mastering one project at a time.

Front Street

I can vividly recall being called by God to the ministry at the age of seven and the call was confirmed to me by the age of twelve. In the beginning, as a youth, I was flattered and enthusiastic about serving God as a messenger because I suffered low self-esteem from rejection. However, the older I became the less interested I was in being a type of Nazarite in ministry. I discovered that I had many gifts and talents that were more appealing than the boredom and strict regulations of ministry. I wasn't feeling it at all! My concept of ministry was being confined to a church like a prison while serving a life sentence to preach. The older I became the more I focused on cultivating my other gifts and the more I ran from my primary gift. Moreover, the older I became the more I ran from the giver of the gifts. I enjoyed the gifts, but I didn't want to meet the requirements from the gift giver. I enjoyed the accolades and acceptance from others, but I was more interested in pleasing myself than pleasing God. For this reason, both my young adult and adult lives were fragmented, unrestrained, and void of direction. My life was rapidly moving from one extreme to another while going nowhere fast. I possessed a solid gift for acting and learning scripts so I focused on becoming an actor. I loved to sing so I focused on becoming a singer. I won awards for rapping and was featured on radio shows, so I focused on becoming a rapper. I enjoyed writing songs so I focused on becoming a song writer. And I enjoyed the tasty looks from modeling so I focused on becoming a fitness model. Does this sound familiar? Am I the only one who is recovering from "I'M GONNA" Syndrome? It is a devastating illness, a virus that sickens and poisons many men. When undetected and untreated it produces a repetitive thinking and speaking: "I'm gonna do this, I'm gonna do that." This illness is highly contagious yet treatable if it is caught in its early stage of immaturity. There is nothing wrong in doing many things. However, there is something wrong in abandoning the primary thing and doing many things for the wrong reason. It is essential that men have a clear understanding of the three m's. What is a *Man*? What is the *Mandate*? What is the *Mission*? When we know and accept this, even our talents and gifts will not deceive us or lead us from our overall understanding of manhood.

Having a lack of self-restraint, focus, and honesty, will cause us to misuse and contaminate our gifts and talents. We must constantly question ourselves, even out loud. "Why do I really want to do this?" "Why am I doing this?" "What is the root of this thought?" Oftentimes we think that just because we have certain gifts it is appropriate to use them immediately. For example, although a five-year-old child was born with a beautiful singing voice, it does not mean that it is time to place the child in a concert venue before thousands of screaming fans. This is ridiculous! And this can be emotionally damaging to the child. However, after a process of preparation, grooming, and training, the child will be equipped to sing effectively and with emotional stability, to withstand temptations, success, failures, and ridicule. The same principle should be applied to us. It is far better for us to endure a season of mind and spirit preparation to help us stand, rather than moving in haste that can aid in our demise. We can no longer afford to continue to live our lives in a perpetual state of juvenile delinquency. Nor can we continue to rehearse past mistakes and attempt to re-live our teenage years. While we continue to live in a constant cycle of regret, our time slips away like the sand in an hourglass. And in the same regard, we must cease from chasing shallow and destructive devices which offer the victim bondage rather than freedom. Like Samson, may of us are wasting years doing the same destructive things and receiving the same destructive results. Many of us are wasting valuable time, talents, and money, gratifying our lust to get what we don't need while attempting to be something that we are not. As we sprint like hamsters on a wheel going nowhere, a nation moans and groans for a deliverer. Look in the mirror and see the answer to someone's problem. You may be the answer to your own problem. While we consistently indulge in devices of distractions, our families flat line, marriages are murdered, communities are chaotic, our children are confused, and our souls become seduced. Once we come to a clear understanding that it is our responsibility to be a source of power for the powerless, then and only then will we have justified our earthly existence.

CHAPTER 2
RIDING SOLO

As an only child, the TV became my close confidant and best friend. I was both entertained and amused to see old re-runs of past movies and television shows. Shows such as Batman and Robin, Butch Cassidy and the Sundance Kid, Bill Cosby, and Sidney Poitier were my favorites. Oftentimes I found that the supporting actor/actress was just as important as the one who had the leading role. The same can be said concerning sports. Although many players comprise a team, there is something special about the solid connection, chemistry, and unity between two players for one cause. Players such as Joe Montana and Jerry Rice, Michael Jordan and Scottie Pippen, Peyton Manning and Marvin Harrison, and Kobe Bryant and Shaquille O'Neal have exemplified this concept.

These players and many more like them have worked in concert to produce an untouchable melody. They had each other's back during times of discouragement and adversity. However, they served as an instrument of wisdom and correction when the other player was out of position. The same can be analyzed concerning the Bible. There are many instances and illustrations of great men who were connected to other men of greatness. Men such as Moses and Aaron, Joshua and Caleb, King David and Jonathan, Apostle Paul and Barnabas, and even Jesus with Peter, James, and John. While gazing in the rearview mirror of my youth, I can now clearly see why shows with heroic pairs were more appealing to me than shows with one main star. It was my loneliness as an only child that drew me to shows with people who were not alone on the set of life. Subconsciously I thought, "Since I don't have a friend, I will watch someone else enjoy having a meaningful relationship with a friend."

As we examine the domestic life of Samson, we will uncover that he was a lonely man who had no true friends. In fact, his only recorded associates are men who used tactics of manipulation and intimidation to get what they wanted.

> **"But it came to pass on the seventh day that they said to Samson's wife, 'Entice your husband, that he may explain the riddle to us, or else we will burn you and your father's house with fire. Have you invited us in order to take what is ours? Is that not so?'" (Judges 14:15)**

Imagine being the strongest and most influential man in your era, yet you are friendless and lonely. Samson was hailed by many, feared by all, and envied by most, however history has no record of a supporting cast member in his life. I can only visualize the inner agony and frustration of having the strength to carry a ton upon your shoulders, yet unable to bear the weight of the loneliness in your heart.

A lonely man

There are many men and women reading this book who know of a lonely man. That man maybe, or may have been, your father, brother, uncle, nephew, spouse, or son. He might be your workout partner, the clamorous man at the local bar, a pastor, a business tycoon, or a drug dealer. Loneliness is often masked under the camouflage of affairs, our careers, and even weekend beers. It is unthinkable for a real man to say, "I'm lonely." Such a statement would cost him his Man-Card. Yet this is how we feel and our hollow hearts echo the emptiness within.

I know many men who are constantly busy. They are career oriented and driven by purpose to the point of being manic. However, there are some who are constantly busy, but they are driven by the fear of being alone. Some are making huge salaries but they are lonely and therefore empty. Some have beautiful girlfriends or wives, but they are still lonely. Loneliness is common but it can also be crippling. It can leave you in a state of depression or it can lead you into destructive activities and behaviors.

Iron sharpens Iron

There is an old cliché: Behind every great man is a great woman. Although I can appreciate the principle of this saying, I don't agree with the contextual structure. I believe that *beside* every great man is a great woman, because woman came from the side (or rib) of man. Therefore, her physical, emotional, and spiritual position is beside her man. However, I also believe that behind every great man is *another great man* because man was created with great power that enables him to push, and oftentimes we need a powerful and masculine push to keep us on track and ahead of the pack. Unfortunately, we live in a discriminatory, prejudicial, and homophobic society. Men are ingrained with the notion that to reveal your heart to another man will be seen as gay. This is a main reason why it is difficult for men to open the door of their hearts to other men. Another reason is that we don't fully trust each other. Many have suffered abuse, abandonment, mistreatment, and rejection from other men — fathers, stepfathers, bosses, uncles, you name it. Therefore, it is difficult to have confidence in another man, especially if that man held an important position of authority in our lives such as father or pastor. As a result, men will trust a woman much more quickly than they would a man. This can be a good thing, but as we carefully analyze Samson's life, it can also be a deadly thing.

There is an ancient Hebrew proverb that reminds us how vital it is to have a true friend:

"As iron sharpens iron, so a man sharpens the countenance of his friend." (Proverbs 27:17)

In a practical sense, it takes iron to effectively sharpen iron. Plastic will not work, and neither will wood. Iron will also beautify iron by creating a shiny brilliance to its surface as well as sharpening it where it is dull. Now, in a spiritual sense, it will take a real man to effectively sharpen a real man. Phonies will not work; neither will cowards. A *true friend* will embellish an ugly situation. He will encourage his friend's heart and strengthen his soul during seasons of sorrow. He will also use truth and scripture to sharpen the dullness of discernment. This friend is committed to doing the right thing and he is equally committed to helping his friend do the right thing. He sharpens his friend with needed rebuke, correction, and chastisement *in a spirit of love*. This is done to keep him from destruction and moral death. Swords are not just made to look beautiful and shiny, but are made for war, and we are constantly engaged in a bloody war with ourselves, the world's system, and Satan. The same analogy applies to us because it is great to be encouraged and exhorted, but a true friend will painfully sharpen the dullness of our manhood. A manhood that is dull from slothfulness, procrastination, hypocrisy, sin, and lack of integrity. A true friend has your back through life's cold winter seasons and blistering summer nights. Whether you are right or wrong he is behind you to push you in the right direction because he understands that when you advance, so does he.

A renegade spirit

Aside from many men that silently yearn for the true companionship, guidance, and strength of a man, still there are some that do not. These are men who are empowered by their own relative belief system of what is considered to be right or wrong in their own eyes. They are under the control of their own lustful appetite and are driven by a force much greater than themselves. They are like wandering vagabonds staggering in the sweltering desert heat, seeking relief, yet when a quenching oasis of correction and wisdom is offered to them, they reject it. They would rather die by their own rules than live by someone else's.

Do you know anyone like this? Have you seen anyone like this? If I was a betting man, I would bet that you have. Now, take a look in front of you. Look behind you. Look to your right and left. Now look in a mirror. Chances are you have seen this man, this wandering vagabond, in one of those five places.

According to history, I truly believe that Samson was in this category of renegade men. These were men who lived on the edge of sound reasoning and opposed any form of chastisement. Samson was the mega superstar of his era. Having true and wise friends would have presented no problem for him. Samson had the choice to pick and choose his friends just as he picked and chose his women. With careful consideration and discernment he could have selected a genuine, strong, wise, and loyal counsel of friends. Having wise counsel will safeguard your life from danger just as an anti-virus firewall protects the life of a computer.

> **"Where there is no counsel, the people fall; but in the multitude of counselors there is safety." (Proverbs 11:14)**

It is unwise for a man not to have a male friend in his life that will always keep it real with him. However, it is insane for a spiritual Navy Seal (a chosen leader with a vital mission) to be without a true male friend. One reason that led me to believe that Samson was stubborn and unteachable was when he refused the wise counsel of his parents.

> **"Now Samson went down to Timnah, and saw a woman in Timnah of the daughters of the philistines. So he went up and told his father and mother, saying, 'I have seen a woman in Timnah of the daughters of the Philistines; now therefore, get her for me as a wife.' Then his father and mother said to him, 'Is there no woman among the daughters of your brethren or among all my people, that you must go and get a wife from the uncircumcised Philistines?'" (Judges 14:1-3)**

The arrogance and cocky attitude of Samson would not allow him to submit to the leadership and wise counsel of his own parents. This was a man who became an idol to himself. He was intoxicated on the wine of his own fame and power. It was natural for him not to serve God because he became a god to himself. Samson was a man who refused checks and balances and defied accountability.

Accountability will force you to check yourself in the mirror of reality. It will not allow you to continue to do what makes you feel good, but rather forces you to do what is good. Accountability will call us to the carpet of character, and then expose any flaws within our character. Accountability will force us to stand on a rug of righteousness while refusing to sweep our life's dirt under it. Oftentimes it is necessary to hear a stern voice affirm, "No drinks for you tonight." Or, "Cheating on your woman is dead wrong." "Man, I don't think you should do that." "Why are you trying to get with someone else's woman?" "Taking what is not yours is still stealing." "I believe in you, you can make it!" In conjunction with a desire to do right, the voice of accountability will serve as a barrier between you and deadly pleasures.

CHAPTER 3

AN UNCLEAN HEART

I can recall back in my days of youthful delinquency and debauchery, an incident that opened my blind eyes in an unappealing yet comical way. I met a young woman who was visually an eight on a beauty scale from one to ten. Eastern features were strategically etched on creamy mahogany skin. Her silky hair draped over sparkling emerald eyes that were soul piercing, as I became hypnotized by the kiss of her bold honey glazed lips. She possessed a thick muscular yet feminine frame that resembled a world-class sprinter, and the way she walked was mesmerizing.

After many long and meaningful conversations, she willingly accepted my dinner invitation. When I arrived at her home I noticed a lawn that was well manicured and a professional landscape that highlighted a beautiful array of shrubs and flowers. As I rang the door bell with a heart racing at a marathon's pace, and I inwardly said, "Man, not only is she fine, but a classy and clean woman. She's definitely wife material."

Then came the moment of truth. She opened the door and my eyes immediately fell upon her radiant smile, her enticing, voluptuous body shrouded in painted-on low-rise jeans and accentuated with cowboy boots. *LORD, have mercy . . . Let the rodeo begin!* I inwardly screamed.

She invited me into the kitchen to wait while she made last minute preparations for our evening. Then the unimaginable occurred. While waiting, my nostrils sensed a foul smell reeking from the corner where the refrigerator stood. I tried to ignore it but my nose wouldn't let me. As I turned my head to avoid the nasal confrontation from the vile smell, my eyes focused upon a mountain of dirty dishes in the sink. To make matters worse, a marathon of roaches were having a track meet on the kitchen counter. They were fiercely racing to the finish line, which were the dirty dishes in the sink.

In disgust and disappointment, I went to the bathroom only to find more evidence of filthy and trifling living. A blood stained tampon was lying on the bathroom sink. There was trash on the floor. A worn pair of panties was draped over the shower curtain. And a layer of dark rings around the inside of the tub resembled the rings around Saturn.

"I'm getting the hell outta here," I mumbled. And I did just that. There is no doubt that she was fine, but I would rather have a pretty woman who is clean than a stunner who is filthy. I can laugh about it now, but man was I disappointed that night! Here was a spectacularly beautiful woman who had a strong, voluptuous presence and a great personality. The outside of her home was immaculate. However, *inside* her home was extremely unclean and could not be ignored.

Heart talk

Such was the life of Samson. He was a great physical specimen of strength, power, charisma, intellect, and passion. His outward appearance was breathtaking. He was the perfect picture of virility and masculinity. Samson was every woman's dream and every man's aspiration. His outward appearance was handsome but inside his physical house there lived an unclean heart. The heart (or spirit) is the central part of us. It is the very core of our being. The heart is more than just a fleshy organ that pumps blood through 60,000 miles of veins and arteries; it is the spiritual make up of who we are and what we believe. The heart is a core mechanism that contains our spiritual DNA; our identification and place of affection. This is why God places such great emphasis on having our hearts rather than our words.

> **"People draw near me with their mouths, and with their lips do honor me, but their hearts are far from me." (Isa. 29:13).**

Most people proclaim that wherever the *mind* is, the body will follow. I beg to differ. I say wherever the *heart* is, the body will follow. For example, a transmission is just as important to a car as the mind is important to a man. A transmission has the power and ability to quickly shift from low to high gears, to shift to neutral, to reverse, to park, and is responsible for the mobility of the car. The mind operates in a similar fashion. It has the power and ability to think quickly. It is able to shift from one thought to another. The mind has the ability to reflect or think back and remember. In other words, the mind can shift into reverse. It also has the ability to shift to neutral and to park. The mind is responsible for our physical movements just as a transmission is to a car's motion. However, an engine is even more important to a car, just as the heart is more important to a man. The engine is the very life of the car. It is both the most important and most valuable component of the car. You can still drive a car with a bad transmission but if your engine dies you are stalled and going nowhere. Moreover, every automotive function completely relies on the power generated from the engine. As such is the case with us. The most essential piece of every man is his heart. If the mind is our battlefield then the spoils must be our hearts. This is why scripture commands us to protect our hearts.

"Guard your heart with all diligence because out of it flows the issues of life." (Proverbs 4:23)

There is nothing more terrifying and disturbing than to see a good man with a bad heart. There are many of us that are outwardly clean cut, driving clean cars, with clean careers, but who are spiritually dying from an unclean heart.

From the inside out

I strongly believe that what is inside you will eventually come out of you. Samson's unclean habits and addictions flowed from an unclean heart. He was divinely selected to be a Nazarite from the womb of his mother and to be a deliverer of his people. When he took his Nazarite vow, he understood the importance of upholding the vow and not just for a span of sixty days, but for life. The sixty days was merely boot camp to prepare him for a life of obedience and discipline in the midst of heated warfare. Long before Samson became enslaved to his sexual appetite, a renegade of rebellion in his unclean heart could be traced back to his youthful days.

"And the Spirit of the LORD came mightily upon him, and he tore the lion apart as one would have torn apart a young goat, though he had nothing in his hand. But he did not tell his father or his mother what he had done. Then he went down and talked with the woman; and she pleased Samson well. After some time, when he returned to get her, he turned aside to see the carcass of the lion. And behold, a swarm of bees and honey were in the carcass of the lion. He took some of it in his hands

and went along, eating. When he came to his father and mother, he gave some to them, and they also ate. But he did not tell them that he had taken the honey out of the carcass of the lion." (Judges 14:6-9).

The origin of Samson's unclean heart began with this recorded episode of disobeying God's law. According to Numbers Chapter 6 and Leviticus Chapter 11, Samson was forbidden from touching a dead body and certainly from eating out of a dead lion. A lion was considered an off-limit animal for Israelite consumption. Nevertheless, Samson not only touched the dead body of the lion that he'd killed, but he ate honey from it and then gave some to his parents. Not only did Samson spiritually affect and infect himself, but also his parents. His youthful days reflected disobedience which planted the seed for an unclean heart. This is why scripture reminds us of the importance of running from youthful lusts.

"Flee also youthful lusts; but pursue righteousness, faith, love, peace with those who call on the Lord out of a *pure heart*." (2 Tim. 2:22)

We should not only recognize and run from lusts in our adolescent years, but most importantly, we must recognize and run from lusts even as adult men. We all have our own customized lusts that we battle with. Sometimes we win and other times we lose. However, the principle is to abandon or run from all infant lusts. A youthful or infant lust is what I call a *lad lust*. A lad lust is a small and insignificant lust that we feed and grow by entertaining its thought. Just as an infant grows larger and stronger from the food that he eats, such is the case of a lad lust. The more you feed a small, seemingly innocent and insignificant lustful thought, the larger and stronger that thought becomes. Like an adorable little infant, a lad lust appears to be a small harmless and cute thought.

"I'll just have one more drink, it won't hurt."

"I'll just take her out one time; I'm really not cheating on my woman."

A lad lust is lethal. It's like a Damien that grows up to become an antichrist. It's like a gremlin that multiplies into countless pests. A lad lust must be murdered at its early age and thought stage, before any actual action takes place.

What you don't kill will eventually kill you. It's do or die!

Every sweet is not a treat

What possessed Samson to eat honey out of a dead lion? This question has always baffled me. It is within the nature and physical function of a honey bee to use nectar to manufacture honey. However, this process and location is not humanly known to take place inside of a dead animal. Buzzards are known to consume the remaining flesh of a dead carcass. Flies are commonly expected to blanket a dead carcass, producing larvae or maggots that completely cover the dead remains. However, this is a unique yet bizarre account of something sweet being created in something that is dead and unlawful to touch.

This supernatural situation serves as a spiritual principle for a deeper meaning and understanding. I believe that this uncommon incident exposed two common flaws in Samson:

1.   Disobedience.
2.   Being a risk taker.

Samson's disobedience was the prelude to a corrupt and unclean heart. His outward ability to eat from something that was unclean reflected his inner heart that was already unclean due to disobeying God's laws. For this reason, the unclean dead lion was symbolic of Samson's unclean heart which had become dead to obeying God's law. Also, Samson was a huge risk taker. He enjoyed the excitement of rolling the dice with his life. His life was his own. He was the man. He answered to no one. Taking an unlawful risk to eat honey out of a dead lion soon turned into taking even greater risks, which eventually cost him his reputation, his power, and ultimately his life.

How many times has this parable played out in our own lives? How many times have we eaten (or taken) something sweet out of something unlawful? How many times have we eaten good food from the forbidden table?

Every sweet is not a treat, especially when it comes from a corrupt source. There comes a time when we must stop treating our lives and destinies like a craps game at a Las Vegas casino. How many times do we have to suffer the pain, shame, guilt, and embarrassment of satisfying our fleshly appetites with something good from something that is bad? Sure you made a *sweet* catch, but you stole her from another man. That is a *sweet* conviction District Attorney, but you sent an innocent man to prison for financial and political kickbacks. It's time for us to check our diets, because we are what we eat.

CHAPTER 4

PUBLIC PERSONALITY/PRIVATE PERVERSION

Both fame and fear of Samson spread like wild fire throughout the Philistine and Israel regions. Paranoia gripped the hearts of his philistine enemies at the mere hint of his name. He was the ultimate action hero of his day. The Bible doesn't give any specific detail concerning the complete physical appearance of Samson. However, assessing the power of his superhuman strength, it is quite obvious that Samson's physique must have ranged from that of an NFL football player of today, to that of a professional bodybuilder. One can only imagine that he was envied by men and adored by many women. Samson was the best of South Beach, Hollywood, and Wall Street. His swagger visually spoke words of immense confidence layered with pride and arrogance. Samson was not just all muscle absent of mental intellect. Remember, he was a military strategist, a judge of litigation concerning criminal and civil matters, and a prophetic voice for Jehovah.

Samson's public appearances before the eyes of society seemed to be flawless. He appeared to be a man of power, wisdom, self-control, spirituality and integrity. However, the reality of his private life revealed the opposite of what public eyes beheld. Although Samson was created to break the Philistine chains of incarceration from the necks of his people, he himself was a prisoner to private passions of perversion.

It is frustrating and impossible to deliver others when it is the deliverer who needs to be delivered.

Throughout history, we have heard about many strong men who were made weak, and how many great men were suddenly exposed. In society we oftentimes confuse character for charisma or we tend to judge one's character by his charisma. We are driven by power, money, and sex. And we gravitate to it every chance we get.

How many times have you seen a headline or captured a "Breaking News" report concerning a private indiscretion of a great personality suddenly made public? Many times I'm sure. How about the award-winning singer who is charged with having sex with an underage girl? The famous athlete who is accused of rape? The Politician or pastor who committed adultery, or a next-door neighbor who stole huge sums of money from business shareholders and investors?

The shock and disgust slices through the hearts of those who possess compassion, however for those who are less compassionate, negative news becomes their version of good news. Regardless of your level of compassion, private perversions of the heart affect everyone directly or indirectly. Wherever there is a direct contradiction in our private and public lifestyle, there you will find hypocrisy due to duplicity. Duplicity derives from the Latin word, "duplus" which means double. Hypocrisy is spawned from the Greek word, "hypokrinesthai" which means to act on stage. Therefore, duplicity will cause you to be double in your thinking and doing. Senior citizens often refer to this behavior as being two-faced. This is a person who changes between two different roles. This leads to hypocrisy. This is a person who literally becomes one with his fictional role on a stage of drama.

A poison within

Men are known for suffering in the silence of darkness. We hide behind a theatrical mask of confidence and character. We become concealed and visually undetected before the eyes of our friends, enemies, and women.

The untreated wounds of abandonment, rejection, loneliness, abuse, molestation, and mistreatment, will oftentimes render a vile poison that will infect the soul and spirit of a man. If prolonged, this poison will hinder full development of manhood and will ultimately destroy us from the inside out. On the outside many men seem to have it all together. They give an appearance of men who are mentally sound, emotionally stable, and spiritually whole. They know all "the right" things to say and when to say it. They practice all "the right" moves and are well versed in the latest style, religious cliché, and financial insight. Like Samson, they possess gifts, talents, and charisma that are breathtaking. However, underneath the outward veneer of a public personality lies the private infectious poison of perversion from an untreated wound. The poison within begins a process of corrupting our conscience, and desensitizing us to the reality of our own folly and perversion.

What is this deadly poison? This poison is called *learned behavior*. It is a defense mechanism and a method of self-medicating inner pain. It serves a distorted purpose of defense from any additional hurt or pain while giving one a sense of euphoria and a false sense of power and control. The poison manifests in various ways: lying, cheating, irresponsibility, stealing, anger, sexual addiction, uncleanness, self-righteousness, manipulation, domination, and deception. There are countless types of poisons; however, the end result remains the same: moral and spiritual death.

The life of Samson depicts a publicly strong man with a private weakness. His unbridled lust for the forbidden led him from one secret escape to another, like a crack addict still pursuing that first exhilarating high.

"Now Samson went to Gaza and saw a harlot there, and went in to her." (Judges 16:1)

Samson's lust led him down to a place of spiritual captivity. He quietly crept to a prostitute's house at night for sexual favors; however his enemies had the house surrounded until morning. This is an example that every shut eye is not sleep and every good-bye is not gone. Clearly, Samson must have had a silent reputation in the red light district of Gaza. Why else would his enemies have known his location at a prostitute's house? His enemies knew his place of weakness. His enemies also knew his lack of integrity. This is how video and physical evidence surface and destroy the lives of Samson-like men. Known and secret enemies that are aware of character issues and addictions lie in wait to expose and discredit. It is our responsibility and obligation to live genuine lives that are immoral-proof.

Yet there are many men that live double lives. They are entangled in webs of perversions. They are driven to taste perversion as a vampire is driven to taste blood. As adrenaline flows and the heart rate increases, every addictive encounter is counted as a conquest. From a collection of phone numbers to multiple sex partners from late night creeps. It becomes an ultimate high. The excitement of plotting, ducking and dodging, and not getting caught in the act of infidelity becomes a twisted juvenile game of fun and pleasure. However, there is a dirty little secret that even Samson didn't know: lust can *never* be truly satisfied or fulfilled. It is a raging forest fire that destroys everything within its path until nothing remains.

CHAPTER 5

IN CONTROL YET OUT OF CONTROL

As if it were yesterday, I can vividly recall driving on I-77 south in Charlotte, North Carolina. It was a warm picturesque morning. My open sunroof invited in the fresh breeze to add to a quiet moment of solitude and mental reflection. I needed this serene time just as a fish needs water because the previous day was very frustrating and stressful. It was one of those terrifying days that haunt the house of your mind. For this reason, the interstate drive gave me the opportunity to *refocus* my vision, *refresh* my mind, and *reconnect* back to God, who is my source of power.

In the midst of being serenaded by the whispering sound of wind and visually massaged by the beauty of the sun, my calm moment suddenly became a moment of chaos. As if 65 mph in a 70 mph zone wasn't fast enough for interstate travel, the driver behind me swerved into a far lane, speeding by while slicing in front of me with the quickness of a NASCAR driver. And then that's when things got worse. The impatient and irate driver stuck his middle finger out of his sunroof and began to wave it as if it were an American flag in an Independence Day parade.

Immediately, poisonous venom was released into my bloodstream where it boiled at 250 degrees Fahrenheit. My eyes turned blood red as steam escaped my nostrils like a raging bull in an arena. Without having a second thought, I violently gripped the steering wheel and turned the Interstate into the Daytona 500. When I reached my freeway foe, I quickly returned the hand gesture that he had given me while attempting to run him off the road into a grass median. Talk about road rage! Man, was I crazy! The point of sharing this mad scenario is to illustrate that although I was in control, I was also out of control. I was in complete control of my car, yet my anger was completely out of control.

And such was the exact same case with Samson, when he found out that the wife that he trusted had revealed his secret riddle to his competitors.

"Now she had wept on him the seven days while their feast lasted. And it happened on the seventh day that he told her, because she pressed him." (Judges 14:17)

Samson's anger-fueled rage drove him to violence; he murdered *thirty men* in an effort to take their clothes to fulfill a bet that he lost. How many times have we seen the manifestation and devastation of rage, from road rage to classroom rage to domestic rage? For many men, the reality of anger is as common as a winter cold. Many are live ticking time bombs with the potential for an explosion that will decimate themselves and others within the range of their blast.

We are angry. However, we were taught by family or society that it is not "manly" to outwardly express our emotions. We were taught not to cry nor illustrate any emotion that could be perceived by others as a sign of weakness. It's interesting that men are encouraged not to exemplify their emotions; however surviving victims that are pulled from the rubble and ruin of an anger explosion quickly realize that it is better to vent pressure than to retain it until it blows. Many of our physical illnesses can be related to compressed anger that also affects our emotional and spiritual health. Women, who find themselves on the receiving end of brutal punches, verbal attacks, sexual assaults, and mental abuse, are unfortunate victims of male anger fueled by the gasoline of rage. There are some men who find themselves victims of verbal fights, fist fights, and gun fights. We are also unfortunate recipients of anger. We are men who are in control, yet out of control. We are in control of our titles, responsibilities, and positions, yet out of control because we are paralyzed by unresolved issues and inner struggles. For this reason, anger becomes the primary emotion from being confined to a wheelchair of pain and hopelessness.

Anger is a silent killer that infects a man's heart and affects a man's relationships. Unlike malaria or any other dreadful disease, anger is often visually undetected until it hits a boiling point during a heated situation. Some men still bear scars of a father who led them as a youth to search for manhood in a maze of misdirection. Some are angry because they see themselves as weak when faced with a strong dark power; an addictive stronghold that seems to have an unbreakable grip on their soul. Some find themselves engulfed in flames of anger due to unwise decisions made based on selfish motives.

Therefore, lack of forgiveness for others and ourselves becomes the life source of anger.

Angry with God?

There are even some of us who are angry with God. Anger and resentment reside in a cold coffin buried in the tomb of our past. However, just like another episode of *Friday the 13th*, the Jason of anger and resentment that we thought was finally dead suddenly comes back to life to terrorize and destroy. It is difficult and in many ways impossible to fully trust and serve a God that you have beef with, *even if the beef is unfounded or imagined*. I believe that there are more men that are not even fully aware that they are angry with God than those who do. The general consensus is that our anger is hidden. It is hidden behind our foul attitudes. It may be hidden beneath the mistreatment of our girlfriends or spouses. Anger can be secretly tucked behind a dying relationship that once thrived. When anger against God goes undetected or overlooked, it can easily transform into malice. Malice is the perversion of anger taken to a level of retaliation. Now, to a rational mind it is unthinkable and foolish to assume that a limited creation can outwit, out do, or over power his limitless Creator. Nevertheless, subconsciously this is how we think when we are intoxicated by malice. By feeling let down, abandoned, or rejected by God, some of us inwardly strategize a plan of attack against God for what "He did" to us, or "allowed" to happen to us. This unfair and unscriptural attitude does not hurt God, but in the end it hurts us. Our secret declaration of war against God is actually an open declaration of war against ourselves.

We find ourselves altering God's primary blueprint for our lives and sabotaging our destiny. We oftentimes think, without saying it: "God I don't trust you." "What kind of father would hurt his son like this?" "I will give you my time and money, but I won't give you my heart." "I will commit to the church, the temple, the synagogue, or the mosque, but I can't commit to you." "This is my life and I will live it my way!" "I'm leaving you."

Real Talk

There was a time in my life not long ago where I found myself much lower than rock bottom. Figuratively speaking, I was so low that when I looked up I saw the bottom. I was convicted and sentenced to five years and one month in prison. I repeatedly attempted to prove my innocence in the court of law, but found no equity and no justice. Nor did I find any justice in the court of appeal. However, God's spirit and grace kept me safe and sane in the unnatural and hostile environment of prison. He ministered to my broken soul and wiped streams of tears from swollen eyes.

At one time while in prison I was so close to God that I could literally feel his breath upon the back of my neck as I bowed prostrate before Him in prayer. It was during these times that he branded his scripture on my heart as I studied between twelve and fourteen hours every day. Worship was always intimate. Dreams and revelations were always constant. However, it wasn't until I was released from prison into the hard reality of a cold world, that anger began to surface. It was quietly hidden underneath the authenticity of my worship and close encounters with God's presence. I did not realize that the one I loved and served would soon become the object of my resentment and anger.

Anger surfaced like cream in hot coffee when I had to endure one test following another due to my past incarceration. I was placed on five years parole with many restrictions. I was responsible for paying a parole fee every month, which is a form of financial enslavement. And I had to confront the prejudice and discriminatory attitudes of society and the church as an ex-felon. These tests and trials extracted something in me that I was unaware of: anger.

I did not realize that hidden behind my Bible and underneath my relationship with God was an anger and seething resentment against Him. It didn't take long for the flame of anger to spread its destruction like wildfire in my life. Like a forest dripping wet with gasoline, it only took one spark of anger to leave destruction and desolation in every part of my life. As a result, my relationship with God died from smoke inhalation. My self-image and self-confidence were destroyed. My marriage was set ablaze and burned beyond recognition. My relationship with others became scorched and torched. Hindsight is always 20/20, but foresight should be as well. It is pointless, useless, and fruitless, to be angry with God.

I have learned and continue to learn that God is a God of love, truth, grace, and mercy. He has no vested interest in doing any harm to us. The uncertainties and adversities of life will come, however we can not afford to hold God responsible for our experiences with hardships. Nor can we hold him responsible for foolish and reckless choices that *we* have made. It is not God who deceives us, but rather our own hearts through lustful desires.

"Let no one say when he is tempted, I am tempted by God; for God cannot be tempted by evil, nor does He Himself tempt by evil, nor does He Himself tempt

anyone. But each one is tempted when he is drawn away by his own desires and enticed." (James 1:13-14)

In my situation, my soul and spirit were dying slowly and softly. I was choking on my own venom of anger and resentment toward God. However, the truth is I was to blame. I was so focused on "repaying" God for what he allowed to occur in my life that I was too blind to see what I did to myself. Although I was given a conviction and sentence rather than equity and justice by the court system, it was not God's fault. It was my fault. I made the selfish and foolish choice to place myself in a risky and harmful situation. Therefore I received the recompense of my reckless decision. This is the hallmark of masculinity. Standing flatfooted eye to eye with society and the church saying, "Yes, I made a mistake. Yes, I sinned, but it is God who justifies me, not man."

True manhood speaks truth *no matter what*. It's not how much cash you have. It's not about how many material possessions or how much notoriety you have. It's not about how many women you have. As one anonymous writer penned, "The measure of a man is found in his ability to stand for truth, and if need be give his life for a cause that is much greater than himself."

Although I still sometimes struggle with the reality of my past, I am reminded that I am not a victim. I refuse to be a victim of shame, guilt, condemnation, and other people's perceptions and opinions of who they "think" I am. Therefore, it is vital for us to release our anger toward God, others, and ourselves, even if we have to do it more than once.

Angry with Self?

One of the aspects of Samson's anger derived from self-anger. This is one of the main components that both torment and cripple many men. We are angry with ourselves. Samson was strategically selected by God to be a deliverer for Israel. Samson was a mighty man of valor who was given the mandate and mission to reclaim God's people from their enemies of oppression. With such a weighty responsibility upon his shoulders, he was equipped with everything he needed to complete his mission within his earthly time frame. Just imagine how frustrated and angry he must have been with himself to know what he was created to do, versus what he found himself doing, *over and over again*. It must have been agonizing to be so strong in one area, yet so completely weak in another. It must have been tormenting to have the strength to break heavy chains, yet unable to break destructive habits. I am certain that it was embarrassing for him to be powerful in his masculinity, yet perverse in his sexuality. Samson's outward anger was a result of his inward frustrations.

There are many of us who frown behind smiles. We are imprisoned by self-anger and shackled by blame. Self-anger chokes the life out of its victim. In silence, many of us simmer in the heat of self-anger while living in a perpetual cycle of regret. Some are angry with themselves for not obtaining a college degree, marrying for the wrong reason, destroying a relationship, hurting the one you vowed to love, not being a providing father, and giving up on dreams. If tombstones could speak, I wonder how many would offer testimony about men who went to the grave angry with themselves? When you are angry with yourself, you take on two roles of dysfunction. You become both the slave and slave master. Self-anger is an issue of mental incarceration and emotional oppression designed to keep you from experiencing inner freedom. A slave of self-anger finds himself confined to a plantation of pain and frustration. He feels hopeless and helpless while becoming conditioned to misery and enslavement. However, at the time of being a victim he is also the victimizer: slave master. Many men punish themselves inwardly and oftentimes the evidence of brutalization can be seen outwardly. We beat and violently whip ourselves with regret and guilt until we become emotionally numb and lifeless. Without visually submitting or tapping out in the main event of our lives, we silently throw in the towel and quit on life, love, joy, and others. The outward manifestation of brutalizing ourselves can be seen in our attitudes and conduct of self-destruction. This can range from alcohol and drug abuse to domestic violence, multiple sex partners, and fits of rage. There is neither healthy release nor relief from self-anger. It holds us hostage without any possibility of ransom until we breathe our last breath in a dungeon of misery.

Nevertheless, in the immortal words of Dr. Martin Luther King Jr., "Freedom is never voluntarily given by the oppressor; it must be demanded by the oppressed."

CHAPTER 6

A SEXUAL ESCAPE

According to God's Biblical plan, sex was created for three essential reasons:

1. Enjoyment
2. Spiritual connection
3. Procreation

First, let's examine the enjoyable aspect of sex. Unless you are a virgin or one who has declared war on sex, I'm sure that you will agree that sex is pleasurable and enjoyable. There is nothing more precious than to explore the fragrant garden of the female anatomy while sowing seeds of love and passion. Sex is so enjoyable that even God Himself allowed it to be expressed in the literary chronicle of the Bible, specifically in the Song of Solomon.

God's original intention for sex was to be an intimate activity of worship involving the spiritual, emotional, and physical areas of man and woman for a pleasurable experience.

Now, this brings us to the second reason for the creation of sex, which is spiritual connection. We are spiritual beings who possess a soul and live in a body. The spirit is the core of you which lives beyond death. It is eternal. The soul consists of the mind, will, and emotions. It is the memory chip of your life. The body is the flesh and blood encasement which houses the soul and spirit. Therefore, whatever is done with our bodies has a direct affect on our soul and spirit. Although sex is a physical act, it has even more of a spiritual impact. Imagine a computer symbolizing the spirit, soul, and body during sex. The woman is the outlet and the man is the cord. The computer cannot be turned on unless there is a consistent flow of power from the outlet (the woman) through the cord (the man) into the hard drive (the spirit). With every new sex act that we experience with others, new files are created. The files are various aspects of the soul which serves as memory. How many different sexual files do you have stored in your soul? Is your hard drive cluttered with countless sexual files? Has your hard drive lost its speed due to unnecessary files from various sexual encounters?

Soul Ties

Sex is so spiritually powerful that it unites or ties together the souls of its participants. Sex emotionally attaches two people by uniting them both mentally and spiritually. It is a spiritual act of giving away a part of yourself that you cannot get back, and that is a piece of your soul. This spiritual connection joins you to the mind and heart of your partner.

For example, you can be miles away from your sexual partner thinking of her and suddenly at that moment of thought, she calls you on the telephone. It is more than happenstance. It is two spiritual beings who are united or tied by there souls. This is why breaking up is difficult because two people who are emotionally and spiritually glued together by their souls are tearing apart. It is equivalent to ripping apart Siamese twins. It is brutal and painful. There is much more to sex than just feeling good physically; there is an emotional component that binds us together spiritually.

There is yet another aspect of soul ties which is a prelude to the sexual part of it: *communication.* Our world could not function without three essential things: light, water, and communication. Communication involves every feature of our lives from telephones, computers, television, and radio, to science, law, philosophy, etc. God even communicated to create the universe. Words are containers of power. They can heal or hurt. They can bring life or death, but more importantly words are an intimate exchange of power. Just as sex is powerful on a spiritual level, so is communication on a mental level. This is why it is vital to carefully monitor what we listen to, moreover who we listen to. Words and the motives behind them are powerful agents that can build a child's esteem or destroy it.

The third reason for the creation of sex is procreation. One of the most important commands that God gave to Adam in the beginning was to multiply. There are many things that interest God; however there are two important things that come to mind: worship and family. God wants to be the object of our worship, and the Father and Foundation of our families. Family is essential to God. He delights in seeing small expressions of Himself on Earth. For this reason, He cleverly engineered the human male and female body to cultivate, incubate, and deliver children through procreation. There is nothing more beautiful than to witness the birth of a child, and there is nothing more fulfilling than being involved in the life of that child. It is a divine plan that we become *responsible* producers. Even if you cannot physically produce a child, it is still your responsibility to be a responsible producer. There should be no reduction in your production. As men, we have an obligation to increase or multiply whatever we set our hands to do for our Creator.

<u>Pro</u>creation is not <u>Re</u>creation

Although we enjoy the physical satisfaction and pleasure that sex brings, we cannot afford to allow ourselves to turn procreation into recreation. In other words, it is wrong and selfish to take something as sacred as sex and turn it into a sporting event. Sex is much more than hunting for fresh game, scoring a touchdown, or hitting a homerun. Many men have suffered severe and in some instances fatal repercussions from using sex as a tool of recreation. Some have contracted a deadly disease. Some have fathered children that they aren't ready to father. And some have found themselves in criminal cases that are sexual in nature. As we continue our quest for more and more sexual gratification from various women, we leave behind pieces of our fragmented souls while collecting spiritual images of female victims. We wound the hearts of women while turning good women out as we operate in the mentality and spirit of a pimp.

When analyzing Samson, we see a man who was commissioned to conquer the Philistines, but instead conquered a buffet of women.

> **"Now Samson went down to Timnah, and saw a woman in Timnah of the daughters of the Philistines. So he went up and told his father and mother, saying, 'I have seen a woman in Timnah of the daughters of the Philistines; now therefore, get her for me as a wife.'" (Judges 14:1-2)**

> **"Now Samson went to Gaza and saw a harlot there, and went in to her." (Judges 16:1)**

> **"Afterward it happened that he loved a woman in the Valley of Sorek whose name was Delilah." (Judges 16:4)**

In Judges 14:1-2 and Judges 16:1, the scenes begin with *"He saw"* but later there is a transition in Chapter 16:4 to *"He loved"*. Now, this is interesting. The first two women he *saw* through the eyes of lust, but Delilah he *loved* through the eyes of lust. This shows us that the attractive bait before Delilah was to prepare him for the trap by Delilah. Samson's unclean heart deceived him into believing that "What you see is what you get." Here is the strongest, most powerful and influential man in the east roaming from bed to bed searching for release and relief like a thirsty vagabond in an African desert. Samson is looking for something beyond sex. If it were just sex that he was looking for he would have found it a long time ago. There is something else that he is after. Sex, as addicting as it was for him, was a secondary need. He was in pursuit of a primary need that was never met between the sheets, although he vigorously sought it in many sexual escapades. What was this primary need that drove him to seek victory over various sexual partners?

I believe the answer to this question can be found in the mirror of our own lives. We live in a world of escapism and self-medicating techniques. Everyone has a desire to escape from their own rigorous reality. We all have various methods and instruments that we use to escape from reality. Some people journal their thoughts. Some workout, others shop. And there are some that even use religion as an escape mechanism. There are others that use more destructive devices such as alcohol, drugs, smoking, over-eating, gambling, and sex. When sex is taken out of its proper context of purity, it is easily perverted. There are many men who seek refuge and use the body of a woman as a type of hiding place. For them, the woman's body becomes a sexual cave of seclusion. This hiding place serves as a secret place of satisfaction and pleasure as they search to fill an inner emptiness. Like Samson, many men medicate their scarred souls with sex as they escape their reality of past pain, racial discrimination, social injustice, low self-esteem, a distorted self-image, underachievement, mental and emotional fatigue, and loneliness. Samson's small victories over the Philistine nation could not compare to the great defeat he suffered in his own life. He could not conquer the idol-worshiping Philistines and destroy them because he was unable to conquer the idol-like issues within his own heart. The earthly timeline of Samson's life reveals the vice-grip of an endless addiction. Time was wasted, anointing and power was spent, and destiny was derailed from practicing the same destructive behavior for 40 years. He deceived himself into believing that his external achievements were greater or more important than his internal underachievement.

This illustrates that your gift will never take you where your character can't keep you. Many of us are extremely gifted and talented, but without integrity we are destined to fail as we journey on the road of destruction. Outward accomplishments are great, but they can never replace an inward character of self-restraint. A gift without integrity is equivalent to a pastor being accused of financial indiscretion or committing adultery with another man's wife, a priest convicted of a sex crime, a professional athlete charged in a nightclub shooting, or a school teacher arrested for having sex with a student. We often judge the success of a person by what they have or what they do rather than who they are.

What does it profit us to be a *public* success but a *private* mess?

CHAPTER 7

SEDUCED BY THE SYSTEM

Before Samson was ever seduced by Delilah, he was seduced by the Philistine system of Delilah. This spiritual breakdown within Samson allowed him to tolerate and even participate in pagan principles that led to moral decay. His spiritual and moral compromises weakened him inwardly, even while he remained strong outwardly. Delilah was a physical culmination of all the spiritual attributes of the Philistine system. It was a system that possessed beauty, an intriguing culture, power, and an alluring sexuality based on occult practices of perversion. The name Philistia, which is now Palestine, meant "the land of wanderers". The Philistine religion was based on their chief god who was named Dagon. He was half man and half fish. His mistress was Ashtoreth, the goddess of war and fertility. Those who worshiped her engaged in the vilest and most perverse sexual acts imaginable. Temple prostitution was common during their time of worship.

These off limit Philistine activities were appealing to Samson. Samson loved the limelight of being the World's Strongest Man. His unbridled passion and lower nature were strengthened by the sights and sounds of this Hollywood-like system and thus cultivated his wild side. This was the side of him that resisted the discipline and holiness of his Nazarite vow and mandate. The Philistine culture and character gave Samson the freedom and approval to lead a selfish and reckless lifestyle outside the Nazarite lifestyle that was selected for him.

Although the Philistines were historically the enemies of Jehovah and his people, Samson's lust for forbidden women and the generous praise of people drove him to be accepted and seduced by the system of the Philistines.

"So his father went down to the woman. And Samson gave a feast there, for young men used to do so. And it happened, when they saw him that they brought thirty friends to be with him." (Judges 14:10-11)

Throughout history, within many cultures, it is common to have a reception, feast, or celebration after a wedding. However, deep within the crevice of this story a revelation exposes Samson's need to unite with pagan women and a need to be accepted and celebrated by an ungodly system of perversion.

It is both sad and amazing how often we succumb to the seductive influence of this world's system. This is a system that controls the *thinking* of society and is founded upon the premise of power, money, and sex. Living under such ideology adds enormous pressure to men and in many ways makes them feel inferior or inadequate if they do not fulfill the standard of society. Those of us who suffer from lack of self-identification, self-esteem, self-acceptance, and self-love, willingly give in to the seducing sounds of the system, thus forfeiting who we are in order to become something that we are not. When we buy into the theology of society, wholeness, peace, and satisfaction will always evade us. Power, money, and sex become the driving force behind many of our hidden agendas and it is the source of our moral and spiritual sickness. Like Samson, many of us have become drunk on the wine of self-indulgence and ignorance.

Living in a pressure cooker

In our relentless pursuit of acquiring more 'stuff' for ourselves, we quickly lose ourselves in the 'stuff' that we already have. We willingly accept quantity over quality. The more we have, the more we want, and the more we want the more foolish risks we are willing to take to get it. Even yours truly, yes, me. I will admit that I have gotten a little tipsy from the wine of self-indulgence. And if the truth be told, even now I sometimes have to check myself from taking a sip or two from this addictive system.

In the midst of self-indulgence, we have become ignorant to the reality of being hoodwinked by a system that is designed to keep men from becoming Men. A *real man* with a *real plan* is a threat to the order of the system. Therefore, in a systematic attempt to keep us in a condition of immaturity and inadequacy, society keeps us in mental bondage by enslaving our minds from the freedom of thinking for ourselves.

Mental slavery is the enemy of an independent thinker. The 'news media' tell us what to believe. The political system tells us who to vote for. The educational system teaches us who to work for. Marketing agencies tell us what to buy. The fashion industry tells us what to wear. And the religious system tells us how to worship it rather than worshiping God. Our minds are constantly bombarded with ideas and images, most of which are negative and sexual. Society promotes that masculinity is defined by how you look, what you drive, where you live, where you work, what you wear, and how much money you have.

We are also told that manhood is based on how long you can sustain an erection and sexually slay a woman between erotic sheets of ecstasy. Men live in a pressurized society. We are constantly under the pressure to perform. For many of us, our acceptance and achievement is based on our ability to exceed the performance of our competitors. It is within the male DNA to compete at the highest level. However, when the focus is more on producing rather than perfecting, then we become the product of underachievement. I have the highest respect and admiration for athletes. My love and passion for football is beyond human understanding. Although I am a die-hard Pittsburg Steeler fan for life, over the past year I have been drawn to more high school and college football than professional. For the most part, athletes on a non-professional level seem to be more passionate about the love of the game. They are not tainted by the sights and sounds of sports agents, paparazzi cameras, red carpet premiers, and lucrative endorsement deals. All of these fringe benefits are great when placed in proper perspective, but when they are not it will lead to corruption through the love of money. The multi-billion entertainment and sports industry gives us what we want, just as the blood-thirsty Roman spectators were given bigger, stronger, and faster gladiators in ancient ages. In our relentless lust for more high-tech and "extreme" entertainment, voices of outrage are drowned out. It is outrageous to pay a college head coach five times more than a college professor. It is equally insane for a first round draft pick to bank a multi-million dollar deal while those who impact more lives find themselves overworked, underpaid, and unappreciated. Firefighters, police, medical personnel, teachers, therapists, ministers, and community activists should fit this category. The entertainment and sports industry bears some blame, however the majority of the blame falls on us. We are the ones who have sent a clear message to the system that we value stardom more than substance. If your home is burglarized, will you call Tom Brady or the police? If a fire breaks out in your home will you call Tiger Woods or the fire department? If your loved one suffers a heart attack will you call Kevin Garnett or a doctor? And if you need prayer in the middle of the night will you call Alex Rodriguez or a minister? We place an expensive price on entertainers while discounting those who impact our lives and our communities on a daily basis.

The fear of real men

Society's system is successful in dumbing us down because we have proven to love it. Therefore, it is an issue of supply and demand. History echoes the voices of valiant men from the graves of the past. These men had strengths and weaknesses, yet they remained faithful and focused to a cause that was much greater than themselves. In fact, the spiritual legacy left from mighty men will forever live in the archives of Earth. These men conquered themselves, then conquered the system that feared them. They were hated, ridiculed, mocked, slandered, rejected, and some killed for standing against a system of ungodliness to release those who were enslaved by it. The entire world moans and groans for men to awaken from their seductive sleep. While we remain in a state of drunkenness, drugs are destroying communities, women are victims of abuse, children are having children, lawmakers become lawbreakers, banks hold us as financial hostages, the educational achievement gap grows wider, the judicial system is unequal and unfair, the prison system becomes a wealthy high-tech plantation, and the religious system continues to crucify Christ.

This is why Jesus was such a middle-eastern threat. He was a real man. He was a revolutionary warrior who was committed to his father and to the resurrection and redemption of his people. It was the religious system that killed him. It was a system full of powerless religion without a powerful relationship with Jehovah. Jesus dismantled their tactics of oppressing the masses of people. They oppressed people spiritually, financially, socially, and politically.

It is time to make up our minds if we are going to live as slaves or die as soldiers. Our children are counting on us. Our women are praying for us. And God needs us to fight against a system that keeps the masses mentally dead in a grave of ignorance.

The best leaders are those who:	Stand tall in the face of adversity
	Stand up under pressure
	Stand alone if necessary

Which are you? A slave or a soldier?

CHAPTER 8

A REBEL WITHOUT A PRAYER

One common theme among all world religions is having a specified, designated time of prayer or meditation. Regardless of our differences in theology, prayer and worship is the universal love language between man and God. Prayer is a time of connection, communication, and consecration. There are countless books on the subject of prayer. Some are insightful and informative; however, some consist of foolish formulas and boring techniques which have little to do with the ministry of prayer.

I reject the theory that the pathway to having an effective prayer life is to follow a 1-2-3 step formula. Having an effective prayer life is simply living a life of prayer. In fact, there are many different ways and styles to pray. However, the man doesn't make the prayer, but rather the prayer makes the man. The anatomy of prayer is founded upon our intimate relationship and desire for God. Prayer is the greatest form of worship and intimacy with God. It is more intimate than a man entering into the secret place of his wife's womb.

Prayer gives us the unique opportunity to have an intimate exchange with God. When we give Him what He wants, He will give us what we need. There are some shallow Christians who confuse fervent prayers of passion with loud and deafening prayers of clamor. I disagree with this method of praying because God is not hard of hearing. Yet some of us believe that effective prayers consist of exhausting words that display scholarly language that only a few can comprehend. This is also inaccurate, because God will answer the prayer of a child who lacks consistent grammar skills. Oftentimes we become consumed by mindless methods and unscriptural traditions that veil the truth that we need to set us free from the chains of religious bondage. Whether you pray by kneeling, bowing in a prostrate posture, or while driving your car, God simply delights in communication. It can be difficult for most of us to pray to and accept the love of God as a Heavenly Father when many of us have had bad examples of an earthly father. Nevertheless, God wants us as His sons. He desires an open dialogue with us. He wants us to tell Him how much we need Him, and that we can do nothing without Him. He wants to know about our needs, our problems, our struggles, our secret sins, and our fears. After exposing your soul before Him, unlike people, He will not breach your confidentiality by printing your personal matters on the front page of the daily news, nor on the inside of the church bulletin.

Prayer hindrances

There are a few issues that will prevent us from having an effective prayer life such as: pride, anger, mental and emotional turmoil, distractions, and hidden unconfessed sin.

I can recall washing my car at home in the blistering Southern heat last summer. Man, was it hot! It was hot enough to make you cuss. In the midst of suffocating from the intense humidity, I began to thirst for water so I grabbed the water hose and began to drink. The cool water immediately refreshed my body as I continued to salivate for more. Then suddenly the gushing water flow began to diminish into slow aggravating droplets. With a look of confusion and pure agitation, I glanced at the coiled hose only to find a kink in the middle. A small kink in my water hose contributed to halting the flow of water that satisfied my thirst. As I meditate on this past episode, I can't resist reflecting on present issues that contributed to blocking my flow of prayer. Unresolved male issues are like kinks within our line of communication. It is the power of the kinks that hinder us from receiving a soul quenching presence from the Lord. I guess this explains why many of us are spiritually dying of thirst in the scorching deserts of our lives. Such was the case with Samson.

> **"Then he became very thirsty; so he cried out to the LORD and said, 'you have given this great deliverance by the hand of your servant; and now shall I die of thirst and fall into the hand of the uncircumcised?'" (Judges 15:18-19)**

This was the first of two recorded accounts of Samson praying to God. His prayer was not one of praise or worship, but rather it was one of need.

Samson's prayer was not centered on what he could do for God, but what God needed to do for him. What a display of arrogance and selfishness! Samson was so consumed with himself and blinded by visual distractions of the female anatomy that he lived a life without prayer. The only time that he ever prayed to God was when he was in desperate need of something from God. Like Samson, do we find ourselves too busy for the one that created us? Do we often find ourselves in tight situations that cause us to seek the God that we daily neglect? Many of us treat God like an airman treats his parachute. It's there if he needs it, but he hopes there will never be a time when he will need it. Yet there are some of us who try to hustle God like a Las Vegas dice game. However, he is not bamboozled by our simple tactics of deceit. It is amazing that God still gazes past our games and flaws to penetrate our hearts with His love.

His hope is that our need to communicate with him on a consistent basis will flow from a heart that needs him more than the air that we breathe. God is more than a parachute; He is our protector and provider.

CHAPTER 9

IN LOVE WITH A STRANGE WOMAN

I may be showing my age a little, but it's cool. I can recall many commercials that I saw as a youth; however there is one which vividly stands out among the rest.

The Denzel Washington of my parent's era was Billy Dee Williams. This tall, dark, and visually appealing Hollywood icon was instrumental in introducing the world to a malt liquor called Colt 45. Colt 45 and many other brands of malt liquor were very prevalent and devastating within African-American neighborhoods. Nevertheless, in the 1970 exploitation age of pimpology, Colt 45 was a "must have" at any party. You didn't have a party unless it was a Thunderbird and Colt 45 party. The commercial set was filled with flashing strobe lights, music, dancing, and beautiful women salivating over the Colt 45 can in Billy Dee's hand. Although this malt liquor was known for its intoxicating strength, with a matinee smile and baritone voice, Billy Dee ended the night by saying, "Don't let the smooth taste fool ya." The intoxicating bite of this malt liquor was concealed by the smooth taste.

Such was the case with Samson, who was spiritually and emotionally intoxicated by the smooth taste of Delilah.

"Afterward it happened that he loved a woman in the Valley of Sorek, whose name was Delilah." (Judges 16:4)

It is interesting how Samson could easily jump in and out of the bed with a harlot in Judges 16:1, yet he fell in love with a harlot named Delilah in Judges 16:4. It is apparent that the extent of the first relationship was based on *sexual recreation*, but the relationship with Delilah was based on *emotional validation*. The first woman probably satisfied his most lewd and erotic appetite of steamy sexual perversion. However, Delilah met a need beyond that of his sexual organ. She filled his need for validation. Delilah was a paid assassin yet she was of a smooth appearance. She was a woman who was motivated by control, money, and manipulation more than morals. Although she was a smooth operator, her name in Hebrew means, "Languishing." It is also interesting that her name in Arabic means, "Flirt." This illustrates that her identity is to use smooth sensuality to mask her ability to disarm and weaken her victim. She possessed the art of charming and consuming her prey just as a king cobra to a bird.

Yet Samson fell in love with this strange woman who opposed the God of Israel and his law to govern humanity. Was Samson so blind by his desperate need to be validated that he couldn't see beyond her smooth mannerisms to see her deadly motive? Was he so wounded from his tragic first marriage that he emotionally tied himself to an assassin just to find love? We could speculate for years and still be without perfect evidence. However, the facts clearly indicate that Samson was on a relentless quest to fill a void and he fell in love with his own perception of how his void was to be filled, and by whom.

Samson voluntarily snatched back his heart from God and gave it to the strange woman named Delilah. He also shunned Israelite women because they were pure hearted and would have exposed his inner issues rather than just ignoring them. For this reason, his passion for God and compassion for the oppressed decreased as his affection and affinity for Delilah increased. There are many of us who can identify with Samson's dissatisfaction with Israelite women of righteousness. Some of us distance ourselves from women of integrity, righteousness, and excellence.

Why? These women require that we become men of truth and integrity. They will lovingly confront and expose our dirt in order for us to become clean. They possess *spiritual vision* to help guide us to fulfill our purpose for God, and they give *spiritual wisdom* to help develop us for God. However, Delilahs possess *carnal vision* to guide us to self-accomplishment over fulfilling our ultimate purpose for existing. We are often drawn to modern day Delilahs because they are women without principles, integrity, purity, and righteousness. *A Delilah will always help a Samson remain in a state of immaturity and rebellion against God, while fulfilling the desires of his flesh rather than his spirit. Therefore, Delilah's presence, empowerment, and significance in our lives derive from our own concealed issues.*

Men, is there a Samson in you?

Women, is there a Delilah in you?

Profile of a strange woman

It is very easy to fall in love with a strange woman; someone new, exotic, mysterious. She presents a challenge to conquer. Her beauty and pleasure is both satisfying and edifying. A strange woman makes a defeated man feel undefeated. A strange woman can make an insecure and depressed man feel secure and happy. A strange woman has the *magical* ability to make a rejected man feel like a first round draft pick. There are many men who are entangled in a web of love with a strange woman. They are in love with something that brings temporary pleasure, but long lasting pain. They are in love with an image of beauty, but behind the mask lies an image of horror. What is your pleasurable Delilah that you often justify? What is your strange woman that you have given your heart to? Delilah comes in many shapes, images, and types. However, her mission is to destroy the destiny and kill the deliverer. Delilah can be a woman, a man, a relationship, a hidden lust, a drug, a lifestyle, greed, pride, perfectionism, manipulation, and control. Her form is interchangeable yet her intoxicating death is hidden by a smooth and refreshing taste. It is always the smooth taste that cleverly hides imminent destruction and addiction. Samson, the world's strongest man, became a weak addict to the kryptonite which was found in his Delilah.

CHAPTER 10

FLIRTING WITH DEATH

It is amazing to watch animal hunters on nature shows who wrestle with alligators, capture vicious sharks, and handle venomous snakes that could kill you with one strike. As I sit on the edge of the sofa gripping a pillow with a vice lock, I can't help but wonder if this will be the day that the animal hunter runs out of luck. That possibility for disaster is what keeps us watching!

In my opinion these men are talented, brave, but crazy. Clinical therapy would be a great option for them to take advantage of. It's foolish and insane for someone to "knowingly" put themselves in a situation of potential danger or death. Moreover, it is completely abnormal to do it time and time again. What is it about these death defying men that drives them to constantly flirt with death? Don't they realize that they are not the only ones who will be devastated by their folly? Their children, wives, family, friends, co-workers, and community, will be forever impacted by an untimely and unnecessary death due to the foolishness of risky behavior.

These present day episodes of animal hunters vividly remind me of ancient day episodes of Samson. On four different occasions, Samson knowingly flirted with death when Delilah asked him to reveal his weakness to her so that he could be captured. These instances can be studied in Judges 16:6, 10, 13, 15, and 16.

From Samson's perspective, he assumed that he was on top—in control—of Delilah; however he was under the control of Delilah. With every toying incident with Delilah, he used the gift of his strength to break free from Philistine bondage. Nevertheless, Delilah had become his personal toy of pleasure, flattery, and amusement. He thought he really knew Delilah, but in reality Delilah knew more about him than he did about either her or himself. Samson became entertained and captivated by her craftiness. The subtlety of her seduction was sensual and fascinating to him. The "cute" death threats from Delilah did not move him. He had no worries. He, after all, had been in numerous close calls and he had always escaped unharmed. Samson was a gospel gambler, a risk taker, and a high roller. Samson believed the bigger the risk the bigger the reward. Total excitement and gratification was equivalent to shooting dice in a deadly game of chance. God and righteous Nazarite living was boring and unattractive to him. It brought him little satisfaction and no sense of power which would inflate his ego and strengthen his fleshly desires. It was more important for Samson to be religious than to have a relationship with God. Therefore, his fulfillment became a twisted game of flirting with death at the expense of his own life.

Self-examination

Before we pass judgment on Samson, let us honestly examine our own lives to see how many of us have or are flirting with death. There are many men who feel empowered by their Delilahs. Moreover, our untouchable and invisible attitude stems from pride and our ability to use gifts and human intellect to always get out of dangerous situations, which will ultimately empower Delilah, but eliminate us. There are many of us who flirt with and tease our addictions just as animal hunters flirt with venomous reptiles. We become enamored with our "control" over a stronghold or addiction which really has control over us. In every situation where we flirt with death and come out untouched we develop a deeper untouchable mentality of being unstoppable. Like Samson, we know our weaknesses, issues, and inner struggles that we grapple with when the doors are closed and when the lights are off in the privacy of our own lives. We are fully aware of that *specific* Delilah-like addiction that has come to imprison us rather than give freedom, or to destroy rather than build. Yet we continue to tolerate and flirt with it like a deadly Black Mamba draped around our neck. We deceive ourselves into believing that we can play and lay in the lap of our addictions and not be affected by them. Just as Samson was created and empowered to destroy the oppressive system of the Philistines, as men we are called to destroy the inner issues that oppress us. However, the unsuccessful warfare and mission of Samson was attributed to two things:

1. His unwillingness to be set apart from the thinking and ways of the philistine nation, and . . .
2. Flirting with death.

As men, we must understand the difference in living in the world, but not being of the world. It is the bling and eye-catching images and influence of the world's belief system that corrupts men. It is our arrogance and folly which compels us to flirt with specific weaknesses that are designed to defame and destroy us. We all have weaknesses and struggles. Your struggle may not be mine, and mine may not be yours. Every living human on the planet has weaknesses and issues that they combat. Regardless of how holy you think you are or how much of a model citizen you attempt to be, you are neither without struggle nor issue. Nevertheless, I am focusing on those Delilahs. Inner struggles and secret issues that we flirt with although we know that they are designed to lock us down on an emotional and spiritual death row to await execution.

What Delilah are you flirting with? What secret and strong struggle do you have that you enjoy teasing? What closet addiction do you have that is an assassin to your destiny and life? It is impossible to destroy an enemy that we view and love as a friend. We are challenged to see our Delilahs as enemies. We are at war! We are in a serious and heated battle with ourselves. We can no longer afford the luxury and liberty to flirt with deadly issues which gain strength from our compromise. It is time to recognize who we are and how valuable we are to the cause of freedom.

CHAPTER 11

A DELIVERER IN CAPTIVITY

As a child who spent countless hours watching Saturday morning cartoons, I would oftentimes become frustrated when my favorite superhero became a prisoner to a villain. My frustration level increased when the villain sensed a weakness within the mighty superhero and used attractive bait to lure him into a deadly trap. While sitting on the den floor with a bowl of cereal in one hand and a silver spoon in the other pointing at the T.V., I would scream, "Don't do it!" "It's a trap!" "She's gonna trick you!" Needless to say that the superhero found it silly to listen to a child's advice through a television screen. Therefore, the one who came to Earth to protect the citizens and destroy all enemies, became an inmate of his enemies. As it was with the Saturday morning cartoon hero, so it was with Samson.

Samson, who was the superhero of the Old Testament, was strategically created to be the defender of the Israelites and terminator of all oppressing enemies. Samson was God's remedy for righteous retribution upon the Philistines and restoration and reconciliation between Israel and Jehovah. Nevertheless, Samson's appetite for destruction led him to be lured by the seductive bait of Delilah, and in the intimate place of her lap, he lost his hair.

> **"When Delilah saw that he had told her all his heart she sent and called for the lords of the Philistines, saying 'come up once more, for he has told me all his heart.' So the lords of the Philistines came up to her and brought the money in their hand. Then she lulled him to sleep on**

her knees, and called for a man and had him shave off the seven locks of his head. Then she began to torment him, and his strength left him. And she said, 'the Philistines are upon you, Samson!' So he awoke from his sleep, and said, 'I will go out as before, at other times, and shake myself free!' But he did not know that the LORD had departed from him." (Judges 16:18-20)

Lulled in the lap

In spite of Delilah's pressure on Samson to reveal his strength in order to be captured, he still found a place of peace in her lap. It is interesting how Samson was fully aware of Delilah's motive to murder him, yet he still found a *resting place* in her lap. Regardless of repeated death threats and the presence of impending danger that loomed upon the head of Samson, Delilah's lap seemed to have offered many benefits. In Delilah's lap Samson found rest, peace, celebration, appreciation, nurturing, heart talk, passion, admiration, validation, and love. Samson could escape from the reality of a cold world that was cruel to him and the harsh demands and injustices of life. The lap offered play and pleasure in the midst of daily pain. Delilah's lap was the perfect place of vacation. Everything that was needed to recover from the wounds of society was found in the lap. The lap was a fragrant pillow which eased mental tension and presented a plush bed for Samson to sleep. However, while he slept he lost his hair, his strength, and his glory.

Many of us have found pleasure beyond measure in our own Delilah's lap. Some of us have forfeited the conviction of what is right for the convenience of what is wrong. The stress and pressure to be a man in society has driven many of us to a destructive lap, where we sleep. Our deep sleep in the lap of our seductive addictions reflects men who are tired. Inner struggles, a painful past, and chasing the illusion of acceptance, status, and fame, have robbed us of all emotional energy and spiritual vitality. So we lie in the lap of our addictions without a fight and go to sleep, but only to awaken to the reality of men who were tricked and have now lost their strength to fulfill their purpose. Many of us have rudely awakened from Delilah's lap to find that we have lost strength, time, discernment, integrity, purpose, vision, reputation, relationships, spouses, girlfriends, children, and harmony with God, community respect, ministry, and sometimes even our minds.

A deeper level

As if losing the most important thing in life wasn't bad enough, suddenly Samson lost much more on a deeper level.

> **"And she said, 'The Philistines are upon you, Samson!' So he awoke out from his sleep, and said, 'I will go out as before at other times, and shake myself free!' But he did not know that the LORD had departed from him. Then the Philistines took him and put out his eyes, and brought him down to Gaza. They bound him with bronze fetters, and he became a grinder in the prison." "So it happened when their hearts were merry, that they said, 'call for Samson that he may perform for us.' So they called for Samson from the prison, and he performed for them. And they stationed him between the pillars." (Judges 16:20-21, 25)**

Samson believed that he could do as he had done many times before to break free from bondage. His past track record showed that he could always get out of a tough situation by using the same talented technique. However, this time was different because he gave his heart to Delilah. Delilah's evil power of influence was predicated upon Samson's allegiance to her during his nap in her lap. Now this powerful and mighty military warrior found himself in a helpless, hopeless, and painful dilemma. His keen and acute night vision, which enabled him to locate and target Philistine enemies for termination, was put out. The hand of power which had ripped apart a young lion and even grabbed the jawbone of a donkey to kill a thousand soldiers was now in chains. The strong and swift feet of a gazelle were shackled. And the one who kept the Philistine nation in a prison of terror was now a federal inmate in a maximum security Philistine prison where he was given a degrading job as a grinder. What a gory and pitiful sight to behold. What a sad legacy to leave behind of a once strong warrior who is now a bloody, blind, and bound man of weakness.

In the midst of his fear, pain, and shame, Philistine leaders brought him before the people to mock him in his condition of confinement. Imagine being on top of the world and then suddenly becoming the laughing stock of the world. Every evil and degrading word possible was hurled at Samson like hot coal upon naked flesh. His enemies rejoiced and partied at the sight of this once mighty man who is now in custody. This episode was not a part of Samson's divine plan. His birth and death were meant to leave a triumphant testimony that would be untouchable for ages to come. Nevertheless, here stands a bloody man who is clothed with guilt and shame in the midst of pain.

We too live in a judgmental, condemning, and unforgiving world. We also live in a hypocritical and biased world. There is no justification for wrong doing and unethical behavior. However, just as the Philistine population mocked and scoffed Samson, so does our society disdain men who have fallen asleep in their Delilah's lap. We are quick to pass a death sentence of public opinion on a fallen pastor, but we are forgiving toward Wall Street executives that have contributed to a worldwide recession. We find humor when a community activist crashes and burns, but we find sympathy for a politician who is exposed for indiscretions. We quarantine each other because of character flaws and having areas of undesired bondage, however entertainers and the wealthy are quickly forgiven and their negative deeds forgotten. If we grant clemency for one, we should grant clemency for all. Our society is far too wicked and unjust to sit in judgment of another. Only God has the right, authority, and providential power to judge. Condemnation and blame is the expected mentality from society, but it is sad to see many so-called Christians who have adopted the same condemning and unforgiving theology from the world *toward each other*. This can only suggest that many church folk really don't know God, nor do they believe in the redeeming power of Christ.

CHAPTER 12

GRACE IN THE TIME OF NEED

The end of Samson's life told the story of the madness and misery of a man who became a slave to his own lust. The latter part of his existence doesn't seem to offer any hope or inspiration. The great and awesome victories that he had against his enemies are all but forgotten. However, the life of Samson is most remembered and associated with the name of his assigned assassin: Delilah. In the midst of Samson's blindness, imprisonment, and embarrassment, something supernatural began to happen.

> **"However, the hair of his head began to grow again after it had been shaven." (Judges 16:22)**

The same shaved hair that Samson took a Nazarite vow to guard and not cut begin to grow again. What an amazing yet strange sight to see: new growth occurring in the midst of a barren circumstance. A ray of light suddenly shines into a dark situation. This clearly shows us that even though Samson violated the Nazarite covenant with God, God still honored his Nazarite covenant with Samson. This is the unfathomable and undeserving grace of God.

Samson lived forty years of his life by his own terms. He used the gifts that God gave him for evil and to further his own career. His life reflected disobedience, selfishness, and reckless behavior, yet the one he offended the most allowed his hair to grow back. Without having a license to sin against God, it is humbling to know that God is a God of great grace. According to the Law of God, Samson deserved death for committing treason against God. I am certain that according to the world and religious system, Samson deserved what he received and much more. However, God's grace superseded public opinion and even his own law to extend grace to a man who deserved death. God's grace had very little to do with Samson the man, but rather the mandate and mission of Samson for God. Samson the man was self-absorbed and brought glory to himself, however the mandate and mission of Samson was to bring glory to God. For this reason, God graciously looked beyond the man to reap the glory from his investment in Samson's mandate and mission. God is like a wise investor. He is in business to make gains not loses. Therefore, grace was given as an undeserving reward to an undeserving man to receive total glory as the God of Samson's mandate and mission, as a deliverer.

Regardless of your religious preference, God is a giver of grace and mercy. *Grace is giving us what we don't deserve, mercy is not giving us what we do deserve.*

New Growth

There are countless men of history who have been brutally blinded and shackled. They have come to the cold reality that God's spirit has left them as they attempt to break addictive behaviors and lifestyles by their own strength.

You may have lost your vision, integrity, and anointing power by the sharp razor of Delilah. However, in your place of pain and shame, God will cause your hair to return again. This is His signature of grace. It is a sign that new growth and a renewed relationship with Him has come. Whether you are in the White House, the church house, or a crack house, whatever you lost in your time of bondage can be restored to you for God's glory! Don't allow the coliseum's clamor of spectators and haters to hinder you from receiving your new growth. Although Samson was unable to physically see God's grace on his life in the form of his hair returning, I believe he could feel it, and so can you. Samson could feel his weak and bloody body gaining strength and the return of his supernatural power. Once he recognized the sign of God's grace through his broken and repented heart, he humbled himself to pray.

> **"Then Samson called to the LORD, saying, 'O Lord GOD, remember me, I pray! Strengthen me, I pray, just this once, O God, that I may with one blow take vengeance on the Philistines for my two eyes!'" (Judges 16:28)**

This shows us that after Samson received the grace of new growth he also received the grace of a renewed fellowship or solid spiritual connection with God. Within Samson's famous prayer he asked for two things for one reason. He asked God to *remember him* and *strengthen him* to take vengeance on the Philistines for his two eyes. This was a monumental request because as men, we don't want God to forget about us like so many have, but to remember us. And we also want to be empowered by Him to take vengeance upon all of the issues that have taken away our sight—our vision and our perspective. Since Samson returned to God and had the ear of God, he could have requested anything in his prayer. He could have prayed to have all Philistine charges dropped against him, or to be released from prison. However, his prayer was to destroy the ones that had violently robbed him of his sight.

The most valuable asset that we, many of us, have lost on our voyage to manhood is our vision. Just as the Philistines savagely cut out the eyes of Samson, our inner issues have also taken our sight. A man is in a pitiful and helpless condition without vision. He is unable to see himself, others, his place of departure, and his place of arrival. Vision gives a man purpose, direction, focus, and confidence. A man without vision will ultimately die. However, we don't have to pray to die with our enemies as Samson prayed in the latter part of Chapter 16. Samson's shame and guilt would not allow him to embrace God's full grace and mercy. Therefore, he died prematurely as a young man without having completed his mission. Samson did not have the faith to believe that the same God who restored his hair and his strength could also restore his eyes. The end of the story reveals that Samson killed more Philistines in his death than he did in his entire life. It is not God's desire nor will that we die with our enemies, but to be empowered to destroy them. It is not beneficial for men to go to the grave with their tormenting issues, but rather to regain their strength and vision in order to destroy their issues. I believe that Samson's physical death while triumphing over his enemies is symbolic of how we must "die" to our own selfishness and unrighteousness in order to kill our many issues. God has a purpose for you and a detailed plan for your life. You may be currently resting in the intimate lap of your Delilah-like addiction, but you don't have to lose your strength there. You may be bound by secret issues, but you don't have to lose your vision there. You may have lost your strength, vision, and reputation, but you don't have to die prematurely there.

Others may not forgive, however God specializes in forgiveness. Others may ridicule and condemn, but God freely gives grace, mercy, and redemption. Wake up! Allow your hair, strength, and eyes to be restored. Our women, children, and communities are waiting for us to fulfill our destiny as deliverers and to break the chains of generational oppression.

GROUP STUDY DIALOGUE

Chapter 1:   **A man, A mandate, A mission**

1. What is your definition of a Man?
2. Do you believe that we were given a specific mandate and mission to fulfill?
3. What is your purpose?

Chapter 2:   **Riding Solo**

1. Why do you think men find comfort in being alone?
2. Is it more or less difficult for men to relate to other men than with women, and why?
3. Do you have a mentor or trusted spiritual advisor? If so, how has this person helped you in the past? If not, can you think of someone who might be able to assume that role?
4. Are you an agreeable person or an argumentative one?

Chapter 3:   **An unclean heart**

1. Samson's unclean heart began as a youth. What are some ways that parents can better equip their children with integrity?
2. Samson did not enjoy the Nazarite boundaries. Do you have any boundaries in your life? What are they?
3. Do you struggle with personal integrity?

Chapter 4:   **Public personality/ Private perversion**

1. Samson looked good on the outside, but was in shambles on the inside. What private issues do you wrestle with?

2. Do you find it difficult to trust someone to tell your most secret issues to?

3. Have you ever told someone your business only to hear about it from others?

4. Do you receive constructive criticism or chastisement with an open mind?

Chapter 5:   In control, yet out of control

1. When you were extremely angry, what did you do? Afterward did you feel guilty? Did you make any apologies?

2. What are some things that make you angry?

3. Do you use your anger as a tool to manipulate, dominate, or intimidate anyone?

Chapter 6:   A sexual escape

1. In your opinion, what is the difference between romance and sex?

2. What stimulates lust in you? What are some ways to guard your heart from lust?

3. We live in a society that is founded on perversion. At what Age did you have your first sexual encounter? How did it affect your outlook concerning sex?

4. Many men use sexual encounters as a "pain pill" to numb them from the condition that they are really struggling with. However, just like an addict, many men become addicted to the "pain pill." What is more addictive: the sexual encounter or the issue behind the sexual encounter?

Chapter 7:   Seduced by the system

1. Do you find yourself gravitating to things or people to affirm your manhood? If so, who or what are they?

2. We absorb trash from society on a daily basis. What are some things that you do to detoxify your mind from the filth that you mentally and spiritually digest?

Chapter 8:   A rebel without a prayer

1.   Why is prayer important to you?
2.   What are some ways that you pray?
3.   Are prayers always answered?
4.   Who taught you about prayer?

Chapter 9:   In love with a strange woman

1.   Have you ever found yourself in love with an addiction or a compromising lifestyle?
2.   Samson loved the sensual and seductive characteristics of Philistine women over the integrity and purity of Israelite women. Have you ever had the need to be validated as a man from a wrong source? How did it impact your life? How did it impact the life of your wife, children, or friends?

Chapter 10:   Flirting with Death

1.   Have you ever flirted with a deadly issue or situation although you knew that it was designed to destroy you? What were they?
2.   Have you ever found yourself being co-dependent on something or someone?
3.   Have you become comfortable with your issue?
4.   Can you name a risk you once took that you later realized was foolish? Can you explain why you took it? What was the result? Would you choose differently now?

Chapter 11:   A deliverer in captivity

1.   What are some issues that have blinded you as a man?
2.   Have you ever been imprisoned by an addiction? How do you or how did you overcome it?
3.   Did you allow the shame and guilt of your failure to paralyze you from moving forward?

Chapter 12:   Grace in the time of need

1. Many people talk about the grace and mercy of God, yet they don't completely believe it. Do you?
2. What steps are you taking toward recovery and restoration?

ABOUT THE AUTHOR

H. Ronald Roseboro, nationally known as "Zion," dwells in many thought-provoking dimensions of ministry.

He is a notable author, poet, spoken word artist, syndicated columnist, freelance writer, motivational speaker, and community and human rights activist.

Recognized for his cutting-edge messages and practical applications, his fervent passion is for the fragmented and forgotten.

This weighty mantle is an uncompromising mandate to bring healing, freedom, and restoration to men and women by empowering them through education.

For booking speaking engagements, seminars, receiving personalized signed book copies, or additional information, please visit: www.zionspeakz.com
Or email: zionpoet@gmail.com
Or facebook.com/Ron Roseboro